# Turn Of A Phrase
## Pivotal Positions in Poetic Prose

## by Branch Isole

*Turn Of A Phrase*
*Pivotal Positions in Poetic Prose*
by Branch Isole

Printed in the United States of America

Library of Congress Control Number:
2010922676
ISBN 978-0982658505

**MANA'O PUBLISHING**
Home of the VOYEURISTIC POET

Order copies of this book at
www.branchisole.com
www.manaopublishing.com
www.voyeuristicpoet.com

The 'story poems' expressed herein look at issues and emotions often experienced, but not always voiced. They engage the reader in life situations of personal responsibility choice or avoidance. This is "Voyeurism Poetry".

Voyeurism Poetry is purpose filled story telling intended to paint images for the reader while evoking responses of identity and reflection.

Turn Of A Phrase contains adult language and themes, some of which are erotic or sexual in nature and presentation.
It is intended for mature audiences.

# Contents

Incubated
Infallibility
Interval Ownership
Kubrickian Orange
Machismo
Masters of Degrees
Matrimonialicide
Millennium Foreplay Thought Balloon
Miracle
Night
O U
Paper Bird
Parenthetically
Peaceful Rest
Pioneer
Poison
PTA
Recognition
Reinvention
Self Revelation
The World's Nigger
Thinking of You
Tru th True peace
Whiner
Winners and Losers
Worship Questions

## Introduction

Never before, have so many depended so
heavily upon innuendo, double entendre
and verbal camouflage to express, then
secondarily to cover up their audacious lies.
The only aspect more repugnant than these
preposterous acts of repetitious weaving is
the speaker who begins to imagine his or her
own vacuous fabrications piqued enough to
be veracious.

In the past this "spinning" activity was
known as double-speak and prior to that
simply, doubletalk.

Leaping back further still we find such
oratory described more poetically as the
"Turn Of A Phrase." Whereby the speaker
either eloquently or by wit and mastery of the
language, profusely and proficiently moved
or 'spun' the topic on its axis. Thus guiding the
emphasis and direction from one pivotal position
to a different point altogether. In this way
changing both the complexion and outcome of
the discussion.

May these short stories of poetic prose turn
upon their phraseology axis' to reveal slivers
of recognition and identity for you.


Branch Isole
the Voyeuristic Poet

"If you can't annoy someone
there is little point in writing."

~Kingsley Amis

## 21st Century Community

Are we truly living
or simply being
Are we growing
becoming empowered
with understanding and compassion,
or are we frustratingly hardened
by cynicism
of a world around us
which we no longer fathom
nor comprehend.

Has the 'spin'
spun so out of control
that we are centrifugally trapped
Caught between opposing forces
as if bound to the rack
Our limbs being torn from their sockets
disemboweling our sense of wonder
whereby we become stoic passive observers
of other people and events.
Grateful,
the closest we come to community
is from afar, through the media.

Our next door neighbors,
the ones our parents socialized with
and our grandparents sat among
on stoops and porches
discussing important issues
effecting their families
are now as near, or distant
as aboriginal peoples
featured in National Geographic documentaries.

we have as much in common with one group
as with the other,
nothing

and everything.

## Aged Beauty

The mental anguish of lust lost
tortures her part of their relationship
as she loves him more, and desires him less

All other things interfere
with energies which were once focused
solely on pleasing him
that she might also be taken
to plateaus of ecstasy
where orgasmic fulfillment roamed free
and readied itself to his beck and call
as tableaus of their love
exhibited in positions
played out for hours

Now a soliloquy
of fantasies whispered
by a mime of giving
they take turns
orchestrating a moment's release
under the tutelage
of what, in the beginning
were the natural urges and responses
of their bodies

yet has it imploded
from love's vintage familiarity
to please

## Aquarium

Water water everywhere
and not a drop on we
One Walking
One Swimming
Two independent species
each on its visiting stroll
another world to see

Two separate environs
do collide
both dependent on air
Life for all, aerobically sustained
through $O_2$ and its exchange

Oxygen vital
with each next breath
for all who would but be
Part and parcel of water
for every creature
within the boundless sea
Life giving force found parcel and part
for land lubbers such as we

Viewing contained
and divided by
a three inch thick glass crust
Are we watching them?
Or are they watching us?

## Attention Please

Artists have four worlds
with which they contend;
First is the physical
surrounding them
The second mental
where inspirations lie in wait
distributed, by trickle or flood
ideas cloistered tight
behind mind's gate
Third is emotion
which fuels production
that composition might take place

from free flowing farthings of tedium
the hours
the pain
the strain
the years

Frustration
Rejection
blood, sweat and tears
Coalescing,
coming together
held up naked to the world

Last, the artist's beholden medium
the Avenue of Anticipation
a moment's hope
for public admiration

## Before the Fall

Please don't extinguish the fire
burning inside me
It is for you alone
my heart's embers smolder
with passion and desire

If you should follow through
on your threats of leaving
the loneliness will kill
what little life left inside
is already grieving

Although I see you standing there
your back turned in disgust
Is the door completely closed?
Have you moved on from us?

Being without you
thoughts bear down
with untold emotional stress
"You'll do fine"
you reply,
"As you did before we met"

As always
you are right
and somehow we'll make it through
but the question still remains for me

Where oh where
will I ever find,
another you?

## Bliss

United,
between a compulsion to write
and nothing to say;
blahg  blahg  blahg

## Blue Line

Four types of people
inevitably become cops,
First are the insecure
controlling bullies
with their insatiable need
to be on top

Their counterparts;
leaders of gangs
the criminal conspirators
they do pursue
But by their behavioral conduct
the only way to know who is who,
is to discern
which hides the badge
and wears the blue

Then there is the muscle,
the associates
of the first
followers and emulators
with little conscience
and far less smarts
The easy way out
is what they crave
it's group and family dynamics
filling the emptiness of their hearts

Next are those implying
"to serve the public good"
In municipal positions
they'd be bureaucrats
Politicos looking to line inside pockets
as elected 'fat cats'

This third group
of blue's rank and file
has a different goal,
one specifically designed
to take a monetary toll
for they thrive and live
off the largesse
of the public dole
What they see
is the government's purse
solemnly vowing
they aren't blue's worst

In this mix of blue
a smattering of others
sprinkled in between
Lucky for us
they're neither corrupt
nor maniacally mean
It's these precious few
who sacrifice
for the better good of all
and they are the ones
who can and should
be standing tall

## Catch and Release

Angling for position
Trolling in search of 'the spot'
Bait and tackle precise
Castings long
Coming up short

Sideways glance
A smirk, a smile, pouty lips
A wink, a nod, contact recognition

Reeling slowly at first
Don't want to lose this one
The dance begins
Verbal and non, language of the hunt

Bodies, Minds, Emotions in play

For you, it was not
"what would be
in our interest"
For you, it was pride
born of conquest

A solitary ride,
landing me
within your net of confidence
Mounting me
in temporary elevation
Portraying me, your prize
of the moment

Filleting me with your steeled rod
continuing to draw me closer,
enduring a false bravado of feigned concern
each time you penetrated deeper
with your blade of self indulgence

Unblinking
you offed my ocular scales of delusion
I watched your use
spawn abuse
until you were ready to throw me back
into the cesspool
of collective broken hearts,
for another chance to swim upstream
against the raging current
of low self-esteem

# Civic Duty

Her task simple;
Testify.
In a courtroom full
Look the accused
in the eye

Tell the truth
as to what she saw
Cite abrogation
of the law

In protective custody
"No sweat"
prosecutors promised

Instinctively she knew
something was amiss
As the door burst open
she took her last breath

The next sight she saw
was the blackness of death

## Clouds

Oh clouds you are drawn
to the land
as a moth to the flame
Ever upward
higher and higher
Collecting together
producing the rain

Some billow
Some cirrus
Each on its own
all part of the sum
At long last
becoming as one

One white as snow
another so dark
gray in between
With thunderous voices do they hark
as if splitting
at the seams

Heralding your coming
your presence
your fall
At once full and mighty
At once not at all

To let down your essence
To spill out your rain
Giving life
to every plant
flower
and plain

This is your course
your being
your path
God has made you
that all else might last

For without your water
your moisture
your dew
None,
no
not one
would survive without you

Watching you race
across the sky
bringing shade, cool breezes
Your sprinkle
from on high
A tear from God's eye?

The life you bring
from day and night sky
From mist
to drizzle
to torrent,
With no more than a sigh
Here one moment
gone the next
As we below stare
and wonder perplexed
We love you, we hate you
Without you we lust
For us in this place
you are never enough
When you are with us
we know not why
When you are gone
we have need and do cry

Oh clouds
full of love
up in the sky
Stroll as you must
Stroll as you will
From over the seas
up into the hills
Drawn by the heat
of land far below
Drawn ever onward
sliding up as you go

Full at once
and then again empty
Constant regeneration
you feed all aplenty

Oh clouds
you are drawn
as the moth to a flame
Forever providing
life giving rain
Waters that stream
from your vaporous demise
are from the river of life
which flows from on high
From the throne of God
does all life proceed
From the hand of God
is fulfilled every need

Oh clouds
filled,
by your rain from within
So is it with us
filled, with our sin

May we be cleansed
by the love of the Lord
The same as your rain
washes clean every shore

### Conundrum

Superior Mothers
The meek and the faint
Offender, and faithful saint
He who borrowed, he who lent
She who was broken
They whom were bent
The graft soaked politician
The murderous Mafia Don
The conniving thieving securities broker
The lying cheating heinous stalker
The serial killer along for the ride
The dictator promulgating genocide
Each and every free will sins,
Together in line
all wait to be forgiven

## Crying

And if the suns rays
should start to cry
melting away the ice and snow
Where will we run to
Where will we hide
How shall the world and we survive?

What relief awaits us
Solace, when will we find
sooner than later?
if ever
in this current state of mind

Spinning
out of control
Aimlessly wandering
Piece by piece
never again completely whole

burning,
cold as hell
at absolute zero
existence is quelled

and when all has gone away
so may continue
the sun's crying rays

## Cuts

once she feared the pain
now she welcomes it,
longs for it,
looks for opportunities to experience it

like an itch
unable to be quieted or satisfied by scratching

its kinetic response isolated

she attempts to find ways to distribute it
over large surface areas of skin
in order that the sensation might become
long termed and drawn out

in a race

as her body tries valiantly to repair itself
she searches for new found places to extract
the simultaneous duality of pain and pleasure

close enough to stimulate
yet far enough away to heighten
raw nerve endings
to a state of carnal ecstasy

disfigurement aside
(and mattering not)
selected regions, hidden
or easily explained away
vie for consideration

open wounds,
similar to the ones
left impaled upon her heart
and imprinted on her psyche
serve to remind her
of the love she has for him
which he so brazenly discarded

the scars wait
for his eyes to see
the depth of her need

self infliction brings her closer to him,
once more

## Debt Free

What will we do
when the notes come due
on the house, the car,
on our coveted
usurious interest credit cards?

How will we respond
to a sixty day pay and stay,
or Out!?

Where will we turn for help
As family, friends
even total strangers
every acquaintance we've ever known
seek our assistance and relief
from the strangle-hold grip
of debt millstones

Who will we sacrifice
or be forced to give up
to extend for a while
the ever growing bills
on our 'past due' pile

How did it get this bad
this out of control
Consuming to impress
friends and neighbors,
those we hardly know

Are we so ignorant
as to not understand
all, must come to an end
No material gain is ever enough
to set us totally free

Our choice one day
will be a simple one
Announce our intention to serve
God or Magog,
and when that time arrives
both will mean death,
but only one will bring eternal rest

We keep consuming
with reckless abandon
things we don't need
but won't live without
Trained to desire and never tire
Accumulating more
from Babylon's whore

Sliding further into debt
To discover our future's
one sure bet
Satan stands ready
to take all I.O.U.'s
freeing us, clearing our slate
If we'll trade our cross
for the mark of the beast
and step through Hades'
forsaken gate

## Dog Day Afternoon

My friend Ed
owns a hot dog stand
and everyone calls Ed,
"The Hot Dog Man"

He sells Brats
and Knocks
and America's own
artichoke wieners
and a sloppy concoction
he calls the 'Mexican Beaner'
Actually it's a chili dog
with a hyper hot jalapeño
designed to create intestinal pain,
Oh!

His partner in this
commercial cart venture
is known simply as
the "One Eyed Stranger"
He wears a black patch
cinched up tight
but I swear I've seen it on eyes,
both left and right

"Stranger" is
dog maker and chef
while Ed handles sales and condiments
Together they make
quite the culinary pair
a home kitchen
dream team
in their dog making lair

(Accidentally interrupting Stranger
while in his dog prep way
I can tell you that 'Yester'
was my last dog day)

## Doubts

I don't know how to pray
I don't know what to say

"open thine heart" He says
"My words will speak to you
Put we two in our proper places
that's your job to do"

I don't know how to pray
I practice night and day

Connect often with the Spirit
for that's what we're told He is
Living within heart and soul
His desire for each
eternal life to win

I don't know how to pray
It never comes out the right way

There are two ways to go in life
with each decision's growth
Our focus, instant relief
from turmoil and its strife

I don't know how to pray
With my life I know I'll pay

There's His way
or there's our way
therein lies the pivotal position
The first step upon two parallel paths
holding the power of life or death

I don't know how to pray
I'm not sure what to say

Planted here by His loving hand
in body's fertile ground
seedling sown
maturity grown
self surrendered
His love
then known

I don't know how to pray
My words they stay at bay

Express your love
for all you see
it's part of one glorious plan
His design, His purpose
His truth and love
for and within
each woman, child and man

I don't know how to pray
but from my heart, I start
today

## Equation

        1  You
           +
        1  Me

        2  Good
        2  Be
        4  Gotten

# Evergreen

Within the hourglass
of our lives
Our mistakes
and errors in judgment
are covered
by the sands of time

Moments we believe
to have been
reliably hidden from view
Gently masked
by the veils of decades past
are eventually exposed

In the same way
the evergreen pine
thrives and grows,
sprouting through
the densest of loamy soil
Blossoms
of sharp tipped reminders
ever ready
to prick our memories
of days gone by

The people we've hurt
remain as dimly lit lamp posts
Tied to us by shadowed
depths and disturbances
of our insecure infused actions,
which violated their trust

# Experimental Jabberwocky Reconstructed

Birthing seeds
of grafted humanity
Rousseau, Voltaire, Thoreau
Aesop, Homer, Aristotle, Pope
Shakespeare, Dante, Marlow

The Beat generation's watering can
Bestowing beauty of Avant-Garde
Intellect appliqués flowering fully
Mosaic patterns
Murals without filters
Adjusting clarity to postpartum shards

Breaking the lock hold of fortuitous acceptance
Balancing upon the spindle
Neo enlightened explosion
Gathering those who might survive

Mass tsunamic tides
scrawling alphabet maladies
Searching voyagers, cove to bay
a labeled home port to find
for limited,
nay negligible,
NAY!
Ne'er a rhyme

## Exports

Impatience; our virtue
Instant gratification; our obsession
Consumers via the almighty dollar
A self-centered people
bound and collared

What is it we export
to a waiting world?
A flag of excessive indulgence
amoral character
and immoral behavior
to be unfurled

# Forgotten

Their service illustrious
for what they went through
Their sacrifice immense
bathed in red white and blue

A background player
promoting God's crusading emissary
Forerunner of what televangelism
might thinly be

A generation plus gone by
old men now turned history
clutching, grasping desperately
to notoriety's identity

Still riding a wave that crested
and now merely laps upon the sand
a faded memory for all
except to those who were part
of that brotherly band

Chained and shackled
by refusals to let go,
to grow
sliding on coat tails long ago forgotten
An imagined time they believed
would ever last
Their once facile appearance now aged
yet clinging to the past

And The World Moved On

## Full Circle

I got one
I was immature
I got two
I was insecure
With three I thought, I was cool
By four I started seeing a fool
Five, I began having my doubts
At six aloud I wanted to shout

Seven through ten, they started to spread
Eleven through fifteen, they had need to be fed
Sixteen through twenty, it was pictures of this
Twenty-one through thirty
it was renderings of that

Then came animals, plants,
ogres, nudes
thin, medium, tall short and fat
Smiling, frowning, grimacing too
leering, peering
beside, under
overlapping a few

My entire body
was soon muralized
All for the purpose
of admiring eyes

I began to feel claustrophobic
like a dog in a muzzle
Covered with tinted characters
I became a walking puzzle

There was one small piece
left undone
A tiny blank oasis
exposed to the sun
One last area
amidst this colored expanse
spread across my epidermal canvas
A single spot from head to toe
the only one,
not ink owned

One small virgin place
A lonely isolated singular trace
Like an island in a sea of ink
Often now I sit and think
about how I look
in the mirror mirror on the wall
eyeing that individual Rorschach image,
au natural

Having come full circle
What started out with one small tattoo
Now again
there's one unique space
upon which others can focus
their admiring gaze

## Fundamentalists

The true believer wants to prove
he is not afraid to die,
yet is he ready to die
as a testament to his faith

the Atheist wants to prove
all belief a lie
the Muslim wants to prove
he is right
the Buddhist wants to prove
he is on the path
the Hindu wants to prove
he can best himself
the Jew wants to prove
no pharisaic mistake
the Christian wants to prove
the Word he was given is true

God desires to prove, He is faithful to all

## Glass Ceiling

Always fucked over
Never over fucked

## Heartache

Tracing lightly
Enough to entice
He scrawled, then carved
on the walls of her heart
bloodletting hieroglyphics
until she was drained
and left to crumble
into ruins of insecurity

## Impending Arrival

We are one, yet separate
you and I

Together from that first moment
Daily you have made my life more,
more aware
more fulfilled
more complete

Our lives intertwined
from conception
Forever connected
from inception

Even before your arrival
Before the world comes to know you
you and I are one,
in love
in being
in spirit

Yet unborn,
unknowing
unknown
It is you who allows me
to blossom, to grow
as you do within
and all the while
We are now
We are always
Mother and child

## Incubated

Like nature's chirps, tweets and whistles
Soft staccato taps, thumps join the symphony
Nearby a muffled sound grows louder
as respiratory chimes
produce a cacophonous melody
Its auditory distortion enmeshed

A beehive of activity surrounds you
Screams from the cubicle across the hallway
tell one's perception of her current reality

Not one uniform matches
A kaleidoscope of patterns and designs
among the cluster of trained professionals
gathered on three sides
of working counters and desks
arrayed with machinery
and digital read out devices

competing triage sounds
of emergency and trauma
all exist simultaneously
bellowing for attention

you stare blankly at the ceiling
unable to move
incapable of speech
lifeless
except for shallow breaths

the stroke numbing pain
obliterating feelings
involuntarily halting
all communication
you might wish to issue

this small world
of medical technology buzzes
while you slip calmly
and quietly
into a nether land of peace

your eyes
the sole contact point
between your realities
past and future


*for CJG*
*~In Remembrance*

## Infallibility

People tell you
what they think it is
you want to hear,
their proviso reasons designed
to draw you infinitely nearer

Within this ill-conceived notion
they then believe
the lies they say
(not hard, not fast
nor small and white)
are veiled in folds
of plausible deniability
and its comfort zone of grey

They somehow think
They're off the hook
so when truth comes out
their mea-culpa response is
'doe-eyed' innocence
with a "Gosh, I never knew" look

When confronted and asked,
"Why the Grand Deception?"
Answers roil in tandem
with their long practiced lame expression
While spilling from their lips
a patent repeated riff
"I care so much for you
I didn't want to hurt your feelings!"
This, their verbal redundant excuse
for all their truth-less dealings

Reformation: I lied,
Lied to your face
believing I would get away
and from your scrutiny skate,
thereby evade or escape
the pratfalls of shame and disgrace
For if you knew
you'd then have proof
that I refuse
to come from the truth

I too am human
and struggle through life
with all its lessons to learn
Perched atop the pinnacle
of the pedestal built by me
I find I'm not as infallible
as I pretend to be

## Interval Ownership

How to be the Big Shot
you're not . . .
Timeshare bought

## Kubrickian Orange

Once edgy,
eventually mainstream
culture's fledgling struggles
generationally delineated,
for their membership
in society's relentless search
not for truth
but for iconic identity,
as denizens of insecure
require
request
rationalize,
Branding

Progressive
bench marks
from bare innocence
no longer embody
pure embryonic creativity,
be it future or retro

## Machismo

Male Maturity is experienced growth
exhibited by responsible actions
in one's choices and behavior.
Not chronology, swagger
the culpability of denial
nor a plea of victimization.

## Masters of Degrees

There's revolution
in evolution
Change
by nature's way
Adaptation
forever in play,
still extinction comes to pass
Being solid
our liquids having flowed,
slowly we morph
into gas

Drifting, aimlessly
earth bound or ethereal
Waiting for directions,
opportunities
to establish a toe
nay, a foothold
within existence

That we might choose
while on the path
one more regrettable decision
less severe
than the last

## Matrimonialicide

There's a stranger in my house
Ever since you went away
We kiss goodnight as you say
"Nothing's changed, I feel the same"
but your touch, caress and lips are cold
yet somehow it is I who senses shame
when your whispered sleep echoes
another's name

Another now receives your best
that left for me
is veiled indifference

What did I do
Where did I go wrong
What acts or words
drove you away
What guilt allows me
to permit you to string me along

Time and circumstance have changed us both
we've withstood the challenges
better than most
I doubt you'll leave,
you know I won't
We started as friends
and will remain to the end
but by your rationed love
now clearly I see
who you've become

I'll continue to smile
and represent you
to those believing
we are not through

It hurts immensely
withdrawing my unwavering support
for my vows were always
more than mere words
But you have drawn
a line in the sand
one from which I will never
fully retreat again

You've made your choices
now so too have I
One values truth
the other wallows in lies
One will go on living,
the other? pick up the pieces
and so it is; in Matrimonialicide

## Millennium Foreplay Thought Balloon

If I continue to listen
to your inane orated dribble long enough,
Can I still get my cock sucked?

## Miracle

The miracle of life is this;
against all odds save one
in a redacted moment
betwixt frolic and fun,
did the sparks of energy and matter combine
producing your chance to eternally exist

## Night

How bright the sun keeps out the night.
How black the sight
containing fright.

Fright to hold back
Who we are, who we are not
Disobeying the truth
In our own webs are we caught.

## O U

The difference between
being lost
and being in lust
is "Oh, You"

Every lover
looks past
familiarity's latent ilk's and ill's
of future's impending
comeuppance arrival,
having long since trod
infatuation's path

## Paper Bird

Origami spreads its wings for flight
each time
I turn on the light
A blur of color soon explodes
as round
and round
it goes

swirling, dipping
in its exotic game
always, yet,
never the same

One moment here
the next
gone from sight
eclipsing my thoughts,
both gliding, different heights

Head held high
Ever onward
through night's sky
Aloft by a wire
knotted and tied

Oh, Origami
might I be like you
ready to shine
in each light anew

## Parenthetically

The cruelty of life
is that we only live once
(the blessing,
we only die once)

## Peaceful Rest

There's no way
we can save ourselves
there's nothing we can do
No matter how righteous
we may become
our sinful nature
still resides within us
Osmotically saturating thoroughly
through and through

Then why not give up
Throw in the towel
Why not
have it our way
Why not
bask in sin's pleasurable angst
Each night, Every day

If God's promise
is to save us
from our sinful selves
why struggle to know His Word

With His single statement
of reconciled resurrection,
is not that the totality
of what we need to learn?

He's prepared to give,
because He already gave
freeing each from bondage
of being sin's willing slave
Why not live a scoundrel's life
and come around with our last breath?
The revelation is. . .
We can!
and in Him peacefully rest

To God
each sin committed
is equal to any other
No more, no less,
a sin is a sin
The point is finally
to come to Him

Repent and change
in His sight
Ask forgiveness
and prepare to see
His compassionate
loving
merciful light

## Pioneer

Like the "King of Pop" title,
self proclaimed
"Pioneer, Founder, Esteemed Doc of  D"
Buying that stairway to heaven
on the backs of shell game thievery

'Peter Principle' pack
assembled staff
Brow beaten sycophants
collectively each on their own
wearily cowering weekly
before the throne
Tokens represented throughout the fiefdom
as if progress be measured
across thirteen thousand days
by those incompetent enough to stay

'Little Bit' attempts to emulate
His adoration pridefully great
learning first hand unbridled ignorance
observing his mentor's caustic ways

Reactive bounce daily displayed
embarrassing those tied to pillar or post
with every, turn of a phrase

Veiled compliments fly, unabated
forefront of this aviator's penurious need
a vampire bat's radar honed to bleed
a soaring vulture eyeing to feed
and what of those, seeing the light
set free from the grip
of this anti-christ
no longer shackled
nor bearing the yoke
of this masquerading
store room joke

## Poison

Trials and Tribulations
Excuses and Lamentations
Peril and Consternation
Caution and Trepidation,
We all pick our poison

Painting ourselves into a corner
Soaring, clearing the bar
falling back to earth
with a bone shattering jar

Decisions and choices
we gladly make
oblivious to the possibilities
that within our ideals and desires are clothed
our near fatal mistakes

Our lives proceed
at our own intentional
break neck speed
With efforts to fill
each day, hour, minute
with as much fluff, flash and cash
as we can fit in it

Through our actions we've courted disaster
as the fickle finger of fate
takes aim directly at us
Whereby we throw the blame on others
in veiled attempts to keep our irresponsibility
covered, just enough

Believing once again
we've managed to avoid reciprocity
by keeping one step ahead
Until we discover
how far we can't run

We all pick our poison

# PTA

Dear Parents,

As we begin
a new school year
It's incumbent from each
of you we hear
We need your acceptance
of our new rules
for your sons and daughters
attending high school

As partners with parents
in raising your young
it's important they see us
unified as one
For that reason
from this point forth
your home values
we will endorse

In accordance with the lawsuit
filed last year
the courts have made it
abundantly clear
Our job is no longer
to be at loggerheads with you
in determining what's appropriate
or within who's view

Your home and you
are the primary source
the biggest influence
as to the course
their budding lives take
and what of themselves
they will make

You being the foundation
of their behaviors and morés
we've been instructed
to assist you in all ways

We can't control
their cell phone use
anymore than we can
your cell phone abuse
Therefore, one-half
of each classroom will be
dedicated space
for egress and ingress
voice text messaging

Half of the remainder,
(that would be one quarter)
is reserved for clothes and make up disorder
Insuring one-up-manship fashion borders
with enough pre-pubescent skin showing
and high heel heightening
to aid at least an appearance
of chronological growing

Shorts should be no shorter
than summer's micro shorts look
Blouses, shirts and tops
no more than three buttons or hooks
For the boys any new, used
or cleanest T-shirt
from the pile will do

And since they insist
on wearing their pants
hanging off their asses
Out of respect for their classmates
(obviously they have none for themselves)
we would ask once again
they pardon with "excuse me"
when passing gases

With fifty percent
of the available space left,
that would be one-eighth
(as in 'eight ball' you know)
remedial basics will be addressed
for our high school scholars
who have yet to pass
the third grade competency test

With this last section,
a final one-sixteenth
piece of the pie
As charted on our colored
bar graph grids
representing the other kids

It too will be fractionalized
yet one more time
so we're able to provide
four whole seats, serialized

Two and two that is
in each classroom's
one-thirty-second space
For the two hard core
on the felons path,
and the last two
getting an education
in spite of the place

In this way our Bell Curve
will automatically adjust
according to Piaget, Skinner
Freud and Bloom
Sealing our children's myopic lives,
and we, our doom

Like you, we will let them
have their way
Then irresponsibility
can continue to play
and wreak further havoc
on a society in decay

Please sign this release form
and return by Friday
indicating that you fully understand
we are now absolved of doing your job
and your children's future
is back in your hands

## Recognition

In the battles of ego;
Identity

Epitome of righteousness;
humility

Kenosis brings enlightenment;
clarity

For when we are empty
we are once again pure

We stand before your throne
sensing our miniscule place
Condemned to understand
through the enormity of your love;
not chastising,
it is a love of forgiveness

We accept with honor and gladness
your command to do,
to be our best.

At once we are awake
forgetting our nocturnal eve's promises made
preparing for another day
of temporal tests

## Reinvention

Elvis, Ali
and yes, Madonna too
flew in the face
of status quo convention
They were quite frankly
the Kings and Queen
of personal reinvention

The Beatles grew
changing music forever more
and after a half dozen years
of being on top
were gone,
while the Stones keep rolling
on and on

Personal growth and its application
is answering a call beyond self,
serving a higher good
than dog eat dog
on the way up
to the top of industry's shelf

Today mere footnotes
of chosen endeavors
enough to be recognized
beyond the next generation?
Never!

In the meantime how many others
came and went,
along the way
becoming spent
As they could go no further
down the path
that would have their names
forever last

'Dr. J' and Michael Jordan
set the stage
for on court standards
NBA types are now
weapon wielding immature thugs
or grandiloquent philanderers

The last time a politician
really meant "the buck stops here"
was with the one who said it
and he ended up out
Not a lame duck coward
like "W.", the current lout
HST was more in tune
concerned with the peoples needs
than a self perceived place
in the annals of history

Economics has always been
about supply and demand
the driving commerce
of the working woman and man,
but greed and cheating
every step of the way
are the pivotal positions
of this world's commerce today

Societies once
were helpful of a neighbor
in both small and large towns
Populations knew
they were independently fine
yet, could rely on one another

Many thought of others
as humanity's brothers
and in truly tough times
wouldn't take advantage
for the sake of a dime

And what of you and me?
What do we bring to this world?
Inspiration, leadership
a search for truth?
The where-with-all
for each to improve
Are we here
for some higher good
and given the opportunity
we will?  we would?

Keep reinventing yourself
to be better, more giving
Strive to be compassionate
to do right and protect
those who lack
Without expectation, reward
or receiving back

Give of yourself
each and everyday
to family, community
in your work, your play
Take all the clichés
Madison Avenue touts
and experience them
in action, in behavior,
instead of solely by mouth

Come on,
grow and experience
becoming a better you
Live your life
by what you *should* do

As a member of this human race
make your world,
your sphere of influence
a better place
Become a new you
brave and bold
without a trace
of the old

Do it,
for your mental health
They did
you can too,

Reinvent Yourself

## Self Revelation

It's all about
the little me

## The World's Nigger

I'm the outside nigger
tell me what you want done
for my life as a slave
is to toil daily while the sun
makes its trek
across God's sky

gazing out, then in,
wondering why

Why some skate
while others struggle
Why some waste
as others grovel
Mired in muck
of preambled ancient sins
to see and feel
life's black hole rim
to strive and strain
to pull oneself up,
only to be
thrown back in

to dig deeper
in this world of inequity
this three plane realm
with its hued lessons to learn
while muscles and joints
through exertion do burn

the spirit's way
of becoming recognizable
his test of surrender
his design
one's purpose
one's "self" to render

regardless of skin tone
to aide, to remember
we each live and die
alone

(the "N-word" is used herein
as an economic condition, à la Ron Dellums,
citation 3; Miriam-Webster Dictionary 2009)

## Thinking of You

There are so many things
I would like to say
I can't find the words,
but You
make my day

Thoughts of you
rush in and out
My mind
is reminded
and although we are
so far away,
You
make my day

Each morning I hear
singing birds as I awake
They tell me all
will be okay,
but You
make my day

No matter if it's
six o'clock
noon, ten, two or four
Working hard
or
hard at play,
You
make my day

Whether it's to the city
or to 'the other side'
Opposite side
of our neighborhood
or other side
of the world
When either of us
is called away,
You
make my day

The things you do
The ways you are
The loving words you say
They make me smile
inside and out,
for You
make my day

When awake
and before I sleep
in my heart and soul
it is you I keep
in my dreams
drifting as I lay,
You
make my day

So my love
I hope you see
Morning
Noon
and night
Right beside you
or far away
You make my day

*for* CC

**Tru th**
**True peace**

## Whiner

You won't let me add another toy to my list
guess I'll have to throw a fit
Waah Waah Waah Waah
Waah Waah Waah Waah
Waah Waah Waah Waah Waah Waah Waah
Waah

You won't let me wear my halter top
and short shorts to school
I'll be the only one in third grade, who isn't cool
Waah Waah Waah Waah
Waah Waah Waah Waah
Waah Waah Waah Waah Waah Waah Waah
Waah

You won't let me go to the Jr. High dance
and stay out all night
now that I've got the chance
Waah Waah Waah Waah
Waah Waah Waah Waah
Waah Waah Waah Waah Waah Waah Waah
Waah

You won't let me date
because of our ages,
the years in between
So what if he's twenty three and I'm fourteen
Waah Waah Waah Waah
Waah Waah Waah Waah
Waah Waah Waah Waah Waah Waah Waah
Waah

I am too ready, to live on my own
I just need you to cover the rent
utilities, food, transportation,
insurance, maintenance, clothing and phone
Waah Waah Waah Waah
Waah Waah Waah Waah
Waah Waah Waah Waah Waah Waah Waah
Waah

I've outgrown the fun
of those irresponsible others
Oh, by the way,
you're going to be a grandmother
Waah Waah Waah Waah
Waah Waah Waah Waah
Waah Waah Waah Waah Waah Waah Waah
Waah

I'm getting married again,
I know it's been
more than once
but I've been alone now
three and a half months
Waah Waah Waah Waah
Waah Waah Waah Waah
Waah Waah Waah Waah Waah Waah Waah
Waah

You never cared about me
what I said or did
I overheard that comment
after my last kid
You kept bringing up
my dropping out of school
my boyfriends
jail time,
and remember
you wouldn't loan me a dime
After I 'borrowed' your credit cards
causing their default
while you demanded restitution
and made me feel small

You pushed me too far
That's why I stole your car
Do you know what kind of parent you are?!
Waah Waah Waah Waah
Waah Waah Waah Waah
Waah Waah Waah Waah Waah Waah Waah
Waah

I'm finally ready to settle down
this time I think I'm sure,
I don't know where
we haven't found a place
probably close to you, over there
Waah Waah Waah Waah
Waah Waah Waah Waah
Waah Waah Waah Waah Waah Waah Waah
Waah

You cut me loose
when I needed you most
Yeah, I was busy partying
coast to coast
Waah Waah Waah Waah
Waah Waah Waah Waah
Waah Waah Waah Waah Waah Waah Waah
Waah

But I'm ready to listen
To change my ways
and as soon as my prison term is through,
I'm coming back
to live with you

I didn't ask to be born
You owe me.

## Winners and Losers

Saw a man today
donning a sweater
PLAY TO WIN
it stated
in oversized letters

Win what?
I asked him,
With a blank incredulous stare
"The Game" he replied

"What game is that?"
"Every Game" he spat back
"What's your game?" I implored
"Kicking smart asses
like yours"

"Oh" queried I
"You're a bouncer
boxer, pugilist
security guard?
Whilst I am but
an aspiring bard,
but will to thou humbly present
for thine own personal perusal
a penned colloquial representation
of officious poetic regard"

"Huh"
he stated dumbfounded
"Is that some sort
of playing card?"
"No" retorted I obliquely
'tis merely identity
for nom de plume plyers
of limited fortunate fame
beknownst only amongst those
in the wordsmithing game

## Worship Questions

Piously he sits
Ears veiled by self-interest
Half heartedly he hears
Listening to a sermon
filled with staccato words
of rapturous righteousness
and repetitious renouncing

As a deacon
he is aware of Father's
painstaking preparation
Exacting eloquent words of God
indiscriminately spewed
to non-discerning ears of parishioners
gathered in the pews

An indictment here
Another there
The making of aural contact
bobbing up for air
as if, a breath of cognition
overwhelms the flow
of disjointed admonitions
concerning man's sinfulness
and God's sanctity

As the pulpit voice drones on
he stares, lustfully
at the woman
seated across the aisle
Wondering, can she be bedded?

Poised
Prim
and Proper,
Hands folded
resting on her Bible
the one auspiciously given,
a gift from her grandmother

Its weight cradled
between her thighs
as if hammocked
in the stretched wool
of her ankle-length skirt

The material forming a cot
upon which the words of God wait,
always ready
to be unleashed

Without head movement
her eyes stealthily glance
ever-so-slightly
slowly to the right
As thoughts of transgressions
bathed in jealousy
and clothed by indignation
produce daggers
of envy's energy,
longing to be propelled
at the target of her hatred

How dare she question my authority
as choir director
and my choice of Psalms?


Mental images trample
the young acolyte's efforts
to recall his cues and steps
A flood of remembered
sights and sounds
interrupts the concentration
of his pending duty bound


He turns to look at the mighty cross
festooned with the body of Jesus
If you love me God
why do you direct Father
to touch me,
with his fingers and his thing?


How can I serve you Lord
and deal with them as well?
They are wolves
in sheep's clothing worn
Honoring you
with false words and claims
lo these sixty minutes
While groveling in the dirt
and mired in the muck
until next Sunday morn

They heed not my words,
nor yours,
Nodding off
Looking around
Staring out the windows
each and every Sunday

Don't they know
I am speaking of you?
As I work hour upon hour
toiling at your task?
Don't they hear the lessons
of your people past?
Don't they care about their souls
I declare on your behalf?
I try to do your will,
and still,
all they do is stray

I ask you to move upon their guilt
and make them give this day
With the pain of a scorpion's sting
to boost their meager offering

May they suffer
for turning from you
and your merciful grace
If they would but respond today
with a collection worthy
of a bountiful passed plate

(That I might use
the reserve this week
and never leave a trace)

Storyteller Branch Isole is the author of ten books. Born in Osaka Japan, Branch traveled extensively growing up calling many places home. Finishing high school in Southern California, he went on to graduate from Texas State University, attended graduate school at the University of Houston and received an M.A. Theology degree from Trinity Bible College and Seminary.

Branch Isole is the Voyeuristic Poet.
His catalogue of work includes books, greeting cards and inspirational gift mats, available at
www.branchisole.com
www.manaopublishing.com
www.voyeuristicpoet.com

**Other books by Branch Isole**
Poetic Prose Series

Saccharin and Plastic Band Aids ©
Comments in Poetic Prose
ISBN 978-0974769288

Messages In A Bottle ©
Inspirations in Poetic Prose
ISBN 978-0974769295

Postcards from the Line of Demarcation ©
Points of Separation in Poetic Prose
ISBN 978-0974769264

Reflections On Chrome ©
Parking Lot Confessions in Poetic Prose
ISBN 978-0974769257

Seeds of Mana'o ©
Thoughts, Ideas and Opinions in Poetic Prose
ISBN 978-0974769219

Barking Geckos ©
Stories and Observations in Poetic Prose
ISBN 978-0974769226

Spiritual Christianity Series

Crucibles ©
Refinement of the Neophyte Christian
ISBN 978-0974769233

Power of Praise ©
Poetry of Spiritual Christianity ™
ISBN 978-0974769271

GOD. . .i believe ©
Simple Steps on the Path
of Spiritual Christianity ™
ISBN 978-0974769202


Order copies at
www.branchisole.com
www.manaopublishing.com
www.voyeuristicpoet.com